JOSH STEVE

A CFO's Mystery

Copyright © 2023 by Josh Steve

All rights reserved. No part of this publication may be reproduced, stored or transmitted in any form or by any means, electronic, mechanical, photocopying, recording, scanning, or otherwise without written permission from the publisher. It is illegal to copy this book, post it to a website, or distribute it by any other means without permission.

This novel is entirely a work of fiction. The names, characters and incidents portrayed in it are the work of the author's imagination. Any resemblance to actual persons, living or dead, events or localities is entirely coincidental.

Josh Steve asserts the moral right to be identified as the author of this work.

First edition

This book was professionally typeset on Reedsy.
Find out more at reedsy.com

# Contents

| | |
|---|---|
| The Unexplained Discrepancy | 1 |
| Whispers of Deceit | 4 |
| Digging Deeper | 7 |
| The Mysterious Benefactor | 11 |
| Rising Tensions | 15 |
| Corporate Espionage | 19 |
| Unfinished Business | 24 |
| Shadows of Resurgence | 28 |
| The Web Tightens | 32 |
| The Orchestrator's Gambit | 36 |
| Unmasking the Orchestrator | 40 |
| The Legacy of Shadows | 44 |

# The Unexplained Discrepancy

The corner office of Montgomery Industries was cloaked in the early morning shadows, save for the dim glow of a desk lamp. A pair of piercing blue eyes peered over the rim of black-rimmed glasses, scrutinizing the rows of numbers on the laptop screen. Emma Montgomery, the Chief Financial Officer, had always prided herself on her attention to detail. She had spent years navigating the intricate labyrinth of financial data, but nothing could have prepared her for what she was about to discover.

The room was hushed, save for the soft hum of computers and the distant rumble of city traffic. The morning sun had barely begun to breach the skyscrapers of the financial district, casting long, eerie shadows across the office. Emma's fingers danced over the keyboard, inputting data into her spreadsheet. It was just another routine review of the quarterly financials, something she did without fail, but today was different.

As Emma scrolled through the columns of numbers and equations, her brow furrowed with growing concern. The balance sheet didn't add up. It wasn't a minor discrepancy or a simple oversight; it was a gaping chasm, a black hole that seemed to swallow millions of dollars. Her heart quickened, and she muttered to herself, "This can't be right."

She retraced her steps, double-checking her calculations, but the numbers remained stubbornly inconsistent. She leaned back in her leather chair, her mind racing. She had heard tales of financial fraud and embezzlement in the corporate world, but never had she encountered such an audacious scheme within her own company. Montgomery Industries had been a family legacy, and she had sworn to protect its integrity.

With a trembling hand, Emma reached for the phone and dialed a number she knew by heart. The voice on the other end was groggy, but it was a voice she trusted implicitly. "Mark, I need you to come to my office immediately. Something's terribly wrong."

Mark Reynolds, the company's legal counsel and Emma's closest confidant, didn't ask questions. He knew better than to ignore the urgency in her voice. Moments later, he pushed open the door, concern etched across his face.

"What's going on, Emma?" Mark asked, his eyes darting between her and the laptop screen.

Emma gestured to the numbers on the screen, her voice trembling. "Look at this, Mark. It's the balance sheet. There's a massive discrepancy, millions unaccounted for. I don't understand how this could have happened."

Mark squinted at the figures, his legal mind working quickly to grasp the implications. "This could be a mistake, right? I mean, it's not unheard of to have glitches in the software or data entry errors."

Emma shook her head, her eyes welling with a mixture of fear and determination. "I've triple-checked everything. This isn't a mistake, Mark. It's deliberate. Someone has tampered with our financials, and it's been going on for months, if not longer."

The weight of those words hung heavily in the air. They both knew what this meant. Corporate scandals had a way of spiraling out of control, leading to investigations, lawsuits, and reputational damage that could cripple a company. But Emma was not one to shy away from a challenge. She had a fierce determination to protect her family's legacy, and she would stop at nothing to uncover the truth.

Mark ran a hand through his disheveled hair, his expression grave. "We need to be careful, Emma. If this is a deliberate act of financial malfeasance, it could involve people within the company."

Emma nodded, her jaw set with determination. "I know, Mark. We can't trust anyone at this point. We have to investigate this discreetly and find out who's behind it. And when we do, they'll face the consequences."

The die was cast. Emma and Mark had embarked on a treacherous journey into the heart of corporate intrigue, where trust was a rare commodity, and danger lurked in every shadow. Beneath the veneer of stability, something sinister had taken root in Montgomery Industries, and they were determined to unearth the secrets hidden beneath the balance sheet.

# Whispers of Deceit

The ominous clouds that had gathered over Montgomery Industries seemed to mirror the uncertainty that now enveloped the company. Emma Montgomery and Mark Reynolds had embarked on a covert mission to uncover the truth behind the financial discrepancies that threatened to unravel the very fabric of the organization. Their journey into the world of corporate intrigue was fraught with danger, and they had yet to take their first step.

Emma and Mark met in a nondescript café, a safe haven away from the prying eyes and ears of the corporate world. The aroma of freshly brewed coffee wafted through the air as they sat in a dimly lit corner, their heads close together, voices lowered to a whisper.

Mark leaned in, his eyes fixed on Emma. "We need to tread carefully, Emma. We can't let anyone suspect what we're doing. If there's a mole within the company, they could be watching our every move."

Emma nodded, her fingers tracing the rim of her coffee cup. "Agreed, Mark. We have to keep this between us for now. I've already discreetly copied the incriminating financial data onto a secure external drive. That way, if anyone tries to cover their tracks, we'll have evidence."

Mark's gaze bore into Emma's with unwavering trust. "You're one step ahead, as always. So, where do we start our investigation?"

Emma took a deep breath, her mind racing. "I've been thinking about this. We should start by examining the financial transactions that seem most suspicious. There's a series of offshore accounts I've come across that could be a key to unraveling this mystery."

Mark raised an eyebrow. "Offshore accounts? That sounds like something out of a spy novel."

Emma's lips curled into a wry smile. "Well, Mark, it seems we've stumbled into our own corporate espionage thriller. But this is real, and we need to find out who's behind it."

Over the next few days, Emma and Mark worked diligently to discreetly investigate the offshore accounts. They enlisted the help of Sarah Dawson, a brilliant computer analyst with a penchant for uncovering digital secrets. Sarah was known for her ability to penetrate the most secure networks, a skill that was about to be put to the test.

In a dimly lit basement room of Sarah's apartment, surrounded by racks of computer servers, they huddled around a cluster of screens displaying intricate lines of code and encrypted data. The room buzzed with the soft hum of cooling fans and the clickety-clack of keyboards as Sarah worked her magic.

Emma watched in awe as Sarah navigated through layers of encryption, her fingers dancing over the keyboard. "Sarah, if anyone can trace the source of these offshore transactions, it's you."

Sarah flashed a confident smile without looking away from her screen. "Leave it to me, Emma. I'll dig deep and find out who's been moving money behind the scenes."

Hours turned into days, and the tension in the room grew palpable. Emma and Mark checked in with their respective departments at work, feigning normalcy while secretly pursuing their investigation. The weight of their mission bore down on them, a constant reminder of the danger that lurked in the shadows.

Finally, on a rain-soaked evening, Sarah cracked the code. Her eyes widened as she uncovered a trail of digital breadcrumbs that led to a name—Nathaniel Blackwood. A name that sent shivers down Emma's spine.

"Nathaniel Blackwood," Sarah whispered, her voice filled with incredulity. "He's the key to this entire operation. But who is he, and what's his connection to Montgomery Industries?"

Emma and Mark exchanged worried glances. The name Nathaniel Blackwood was not one they recognized from within the company, and it raised more questions than answers.

"We need to find out everything we can about Nathaniel Blackwood," Emma said with determination. "This is just the beginning, and I fear we've stepped into a web of deceit that's far more intricate than we could have ever imagined."

As the rain continued to pour outside, the trio knew that they were delving deeper into a mystery that threatened not only the financial stability of Montgomery Industries but also their own safety. Nathaniel Blackwood remained a shadowy figure, lurking at the heart of a corporate conspiracy that had only just begun to unravel.

# Digging Deeper

The rain that had soaked the city for days seemed to mirror the unrelenting persistence of Emma, Mark, and Sarah as they delved deeper into the enigma surrounding Nathaniel Blackwood and the financial discrepancies plaguing Montgomery Industries. The trio had become an unlikely team of investigators, navigating the treacherous waters of corporate intrigue with each keystroke, and the stakes had never been higher.

Sarah's cramped basement apartment had transformed into their makeshift headquarters. Banks of computer screens cast an eerie blue glow, illuminating the room with a surreal ambiance. It was here, amidst the hum of machines and the scent of takeaway pizza boxes, that they pieced together the fragments of their investigation.

Emma sat at the center of the operation, her eyes scanning through pages of financial records. "Nathaniel Blackwood," she muttered, as if the name held the key to unlocking the entire puzzle. "We know he's linked to those offshore accounts, but who is he, and why is he doing this?"

Mark, leaning over Emma's shoulder, sifted through the documents with furrowed brows. "I've checked our employee database, and there's no record of a Nathaniel Blackwood ever working at Montgomery Industries. This person seems to have come out of nowhere."

Sarah, immersed in her own digital world, suddenly perked up. "I've found something, guys. Nathaniel Blackwood has a history, but it's buried deep. It looks like he's a master at erasing his tracks."

Emma leaned forward, her eyes narrowing. "Tell us everything you've found, Sarah."

With a few clicks, Sarah projected a timeline of Nathaniel Blackwood's digital footprint on the screens. "It seems he's been involved in some shady financial dealings for years. Money laundering, offshore accounts, you name it. But there's one peculiar thing—his involvement with different companies, always behind the scenes."

Mark raised an eyebrow. "So, he's a financial puppeteer, pulling the strings from the shadows?"

Sarah nodded. "Exactly. But what's intriguing is that his name has never surfaced in any corporate investigation. It's as if he's immune to scrutiny."

Emma's mind raced as she considered the implications. "Could he be using a false identity? And if so, why would he target Montgomery Industries?"

Mark leaned back, deep in thought. "We need to find a way to unmask him. If we can expose Nathaniel Blackwood's true identity and motives, we might finally get to the bottom of this."

The room fell silent as the weight of their mission settled upon them. But silence was a luxury they couldn't afford for long. As they continued to dig through the data, Emma's phone buzzed with an incoming call. She glanced at the screen and recognized the number—it was from her father, Charles Montgomery, the company's founder.

"Excuse me," Emma said, stepping out of the room to take the call. The voices of Mark and Sarah were muffled as she closed the door behind her.

"Emma," her father's voice sounded strained. "I've just received an anonymous letter. It contains information about our financial discrepancies and warns of dire consequences if we don't comply with the sender's demands."

Emma's heart raced. The threat had escalated, and the company's reputation was hanging by a thread. "Dad, we're already investigating this. We'll get to the bottom of it. Do not comply with their demands."

Charles Montgomery hesitated, his concern evident. "I trust you, Emma, but be careful. Whoever is behind this is playing a dangerous game."

As the call ended, Emma's resolve hardened. She rejoined Mark and Sarah, her expression determined. "We're running out of time. The anonymous sender is pushing us to act. We need to find out who Nathaniel Blackwood is, and fast."

Sarah continued to sift through data, her fingers flying across the keyboard. "I've been tracing Blackwood's online presence, and I think I've found a lead. He's left a trail of breadcrumbs through encrypted chat rooms frequented by financial criminals. I'm trying to access a live conversation now."

Minutes felt like hours as Sarah worked her magic. The room held its collective breath until a message appeared on the screen: "Nathaniel_Blackwood: Meeting tonight at the RedStar Lounge. Midnight."

Emma's heart raced as she read the message aloud. "A meeting tonight, at the RedStar Lounge. This could be our chance to finally confront Nathaniel Blackwood face-to-face."

Mark's eyes gleamed with a mix of determination and caution. "We can't walk into this blindly, Emma. We need a plan."

Emma nodded, her mind racing. "We'll need to be discreet, blend in with the crowd. Sarah, can you find out more about the RedStar Lounge? Who frequents it? What kind of clientele do they have?"

Sarah nodded and got to work, her fingers dancing over the keyboard once again. "I'll do my best, Emma."

As the clock ticked towards midnight, the trio prepared for a meeting that held the promise of answers but also the peril of the unknown. They had entered a world of shadows, where the line between ally and adversary was blurred, and where the truth remained buried beneath layers of deceit. The RedStar Lounge awaited, and with it, the next chapter in their relentless pursuit of justice and redemption.

# The Mysterious Benefactor

The RedStar Lounge, nestled in a forgotten corner of the city's nightlife, was a realm of dimly lit extravagance. Its velvet-lined booths and low-hanging chandeliers exuded an air of opulence, but beneath the surface, it harbored secrets darker than the night itself. As Emma, Mark, and Sarah entered the lounge, they couldn't help but feel like intruders in this realm of decadence.

Emma had chosen a conservative black dress to blend in, her fiery determination hidden beneath a facade of poise. Mark, in a tailored suit, exuded a sense of authority, while Sarah, disguised as a tech-savvy partygoer, clutched a smartphone like a lifeline. They had rehearsed their cover stories, ready to infiltrate the meeting where Nathaniel Blackwood was rumored to appear.

The lounge was filled with patrons engaged in hushed conversations. Jazz music drifted from a corner stage, where a sultry singer crooned melancholic melodies. The trio made their way to the bar, scanning the crowd for any signs of their mysterious benefactor.

"I've done some digging," Sarah whispered to Emma, "and it seems the RedStar Lounge is known for hosting discreet gatherings of the city's elite. If Nathaniel Blackwood is here, he's likely in one of the private rooms."

Emma nodded, her eyes scanning the lounge. "Keep an eye out for any unusual activity. We need to find him before he realizes we're onto him."

As they lingered near the bar, sipping cocktails and engaging in casual conversation with nearby patrons, Mark's keen eye caught sight of a man who seemed out of place. Dressed in a sleek black suit, he sat alone at a corner table, a glass of scotch in hand, his eyes scanning the room with a calculating gaze.

Mark nudged Emma discreetly and inclined his head in the man's direction. "Emma, take a look at that guy in the corner. He's been watching us."

Emma followed Mark's gaze and studied the man for a moment. "Could that be Nathaniel Blackwood?"

Mark nodded, his voice barely audible. "It's possible. We should get closer and see if we can hear anything."

With practiced nonchalance, they moved closer to the corner table, positioning themselves at a nearby booth where they could eavesdrop without appearing conspicuous. Sarah discreetly adjusted the recording app on her smartphone.

The man in the black suit leaned forward, engaged in conversation with a well-dressed woman who appeared equally enigmatic. Their voices were low, and the trio strained to catch every word.

"I assure you, Mr. Blackwood, the funds have been discreetly transferred as per your instructions," the woman said, her tone tinged with apprehension.

Nathaniel Blackwood, his face partially obscured by the dim lighting, nodded. "Good. Our plan is proceeding as expected. They won't see it coming."

Emma exchanged a silent glance with Mark, her heart pounding. This was it—they were close to unraveling the mystery. But they needed more information.

Sarah discreetly signaled to the others that she was recording the conversation. Emma and Mark leaned in, attempting to gather as much information as possible.

Nathaniel Blackwood continued, "Make sure the board approves the merger, no matter what it takes. Once we control Montgomery Industries, our influence in the market will be unparalleled."

Emma's eyes widened in shock. The pieces of the puzzle were falling into place. Blackwood was orchestrating a hostile takeover of the company, and he had insider help to ensure its success.

The woman leaned closer, her voice almost a whisper. "What about Emma Montgomery? She's been digging into our affairs. Should we be concerned?"

Nathaniel Blackwood's lips curled into a sinister smile. "Emma Montgomery is a thorn in our side, but she won't be a problem for much longer. I have a plan in motion to discredit her and force her out of the company."

Mark clenched his fists, his face a mask of anger and determination. They had to expose Blackwood's plan and protect Emma before it was too late.

Before they could react, their cover was blown. A tall, burly man in a dark suit approached their booth, his eyes cold and calculating. "May I help you?" he asked, his voice laced with thinly veiled menace.

Emma, Mark, and Sarah exchanged uneasy glances. Their mission had taken an unexpected turn, and the enemy was now aware of their presence. The RedStar Lounge, once a haven of luxury and intrigue, had become a perilous battleground where secrets and lies collided.

As the tension in the lounge reached its zenith, the trio had a split-second decision to make—retreat and regroup, or confront Nathaniel Blackwood and his sinister plot head-on. The fate of Montgomery Industries hung in the balance, and the next move they made could determine whether they emerged victorious or fell victim to the web of deceit that had ensnared them all.

# Rising Tensions

The RedStar Lounge had transformed from a realm of decadence into a battleground of tension and uncertainty. Emma, Mark, and Sarah found themselves cornered, their encounter with Nathaniel Blackwood's enigmatic associate leaving them with no choice but to regroup and rethink their strategy.

As they exited the lounge, Emma could feel the weight of the situation pressing down on her. "We need to get out of here," she whispered to her companions. "Blackwood knows we're onto him, and we can't confront him directly in this crowded place."

Mark nodded in agreement. "We'll head back to Sarah's apartment. It's our safest option for now. We need to analyze the information we gathered and figure out our next move."

Their footsteps echoed in the dimly lit alley outside the lounge as they made their way to their waiting car. The night air was thick with tension, and the distant sounds of sirens and car horns served as a haunting backdrop to their thoughts.

Once back at Sarah's apartment, they gathered around her computer screens, replaying the recording of Nathaniel Blackwood's conversation. Every word, every inflection was scrutinized as they tried to piece together the puzzle.

"Did you catch that part about discrediting me?" Emma asked, her voice tight with concern. "He's planning to force me out of Montgomery Industries. We can't let that happen."

Mark, his expression grave, nodded. "We also learned about their intention to ensure the board approves a merger. That could be the final blow to our company."

Sarah interjected, her fingers dancing over the keyboard as she cross-referenced the information they had gathered. "I've been digging deeper into Blackwood's connections. It seems he has a network of financial associates, some of whom are influential members of the board."

Emma's eyes narrowed. "So, they're infiltrating our board to manipulate the merger decision from within. But who are these insiders, and how do they benefit from this?"

Mark leaned back in his chair, deep in thought. "We need to identify the individuals involved and gather evidence of their complicity. That's the only way we can stop Blackwood's plan."

Sarah, her gaze focused on the screen, piped up, "I might have a lead on one of the insiders. A certain board member, Anthony Winters, has had a series of unusual financial transactions in recent months. It's worth looking into."

Emma's resolve hardened. "Let's start there, then. We need to discreetly investigate Anthony Winters and find out if he's involved with Blackwood. If we can expose one of the insiders, we might be able to disrupt Blackwood's plan."

Over the next few days, the trio began their covert investigation into Anthony

Winters. They combed through financial records, interviewed discreet sources, and analyzed the connections that seemed to lead to him. As the pieces of the puzzle fell into place, a picture of deceit and manipulation emerged.

It became clear that Winters had been involved in a series of shady financial deals that directly benefited Blackwood's plan for the hostile takeover of Montgomery Industries. But they needed concrete evidence to prove Winters' involvement and to convince the board of the looming threat.

One evening, as Emma and Mark discussed their findings in her office at Montgomery Industries, a knock on the door interrupted their conversation. Startled, they exchanged puzzled glances before Emma called out, "Come in."

The door opened, and Anthony Winters stepped inside, his demeanor strangely composed. "Emma, Mark, I couldn't help but overhear your conversation. It seems you've been digging into my affairs."

Emma's heart raced as she assessed the situation. Winters' intrusion was unexpected, and they needed to tread carefully.

Mark, his voice steady, responded, "Mr. Winters, we have reason to believe that there are irregularities in your financial transactions that require further examination. This is a confidential matter, and we are conducting an internal investigation."

Winters raised an eyebrow, his lips curling into a disarming smile. "Well, I can assure you that there's a perfectly reasonable explanation for those transactions. There's no need for an investigation."

Emma knew they couldn't back down now. She leaned forward, her eyes locked with Winters'. "Mr. Winters, our duty is to protect the best interests of Montgomery Industries and its shareholders. If you have nothing to hide, then you have nothing to fear from this investigation."

Winters' smile faded, replaced by a cold, calculating look. "Very well, Emma. But be careful. Sometimes, digging too deep can lead to unintended consequences."

As Winters left the office, Emma couldn't shake the feeling that they were getting closer to exposing the truth, but they were also inching closer to danger. The rising tensions within the company were palpable, and their adversaries were becoming increasingly desperate.

Back in Sarah's apartment, they continued their investigation, determined to gather the evidence they needed to expose Anthony Winters and thwart Nathaniel Blackwood's sinister plot. The stakes were higher than ever, and with each revelation, they found themselves deeper in a web of deception and intrigue. But they had come too far to turn back now, and the battle for the soul of Montgomery Industries was far from over.

# Corporate Espionage

In the dimly lit basement of Sarah Dawson's apartment, the trio of Emma, Mark, and Sarah continued their clandestine investigation into Anthony Winters and Nathaniel Blackwood. The tension in the room was palpable as they dissected the information they had gathered, piecing together a mosaic of deceit that threatened to consume Montgomery Industries.

Sarah, her fingers flying across the keyboard, had become their digital sleuth, unearthing the buried secrets of Anthony Winters. "I've managed to trace some of Winters' offshore accounts to shell companies," she reported. "It looks like he's been funneling money through a complex network to disguise his involvement."

Emma nodded, her eyes glued to the screens displaying financial transactions and corporate records. "This is a deliberate attempt to hide his connections with Blackwood. We need concrete evidence of their collusion if we're going to expose them."

Mark leaned forward, a determined glint in his eyes. "I've been looking into Winters' recent meetings and interactions within the company. He's been in contact with several board members who have a history of supporting Blackwood's agenda. We might be able to leverage this information."

As they brainstormed their next move, Emma's phone buzzed with a message from an unknown number. She furrowed her brow as she read the message: "You're getting closer, but you're not alone in this. Meet me tonight at the city's abandoned subway station at midnight if you want the truth."

Emma's heart raced as she shared the message with her companions. The prospect of a clandestine meeting with an unknown ally was both exhilarating and treacherous. They had to make a choice—trust the message and take the risk or continue their investigation from the shadows.

After much debate, they decided to accept the invitation. Emma, Mark, and Sarah donned dark clothing and made their way to the abandoned subway station, their footsteps echoing in the eerie silence of the underground tunnels. Graffiti-covered walls bore witness to the passage of time, and the flickering overhead lights cast long, ominous shadows.

As they reached the designated meeting point, they saw a lone figure shrouded in darkness. The stranger stepped forward, revealing a face concealed by a mask.

"You must be Emma Montgomery," the masked figure said, their voice low and distorted. "I've been watching your investigation closely. I have information that could help you expose Anthony Winters and Nathaniel Blackwood."

Emma nodded, her voice steady despite her unease. "We need all the help we can get. What do you know?"

The masked figure handed over a USB drive. "This contains evidence of their financial transactions, emails, and correspondence that will tie Winters and Blackwood to their plot against Montgomery Industries. Use it wisely."

Mark accepted the USB drive, his eyes never leaving the masked figure. "Who are you, and why are you helping us?"

The figure hesitated for a moment before replying, "I have my reasons for opposing Blackwood's plan, and I believe in justice. But remember, the deeper you go, the more dangerous it becomes. Trust no one."

With that ominous warning, the masked figure disappeared into the shadows of the subway station, leaving Emma, Mark, and Sarah with a newfound sense of urgency. They knew that their investigation had just taken a treacherous turn, and they had to act quickly to make use of the information they had received.

Back in Sarah's apartment, they analyzed the contents of the USB drive, uncovering a trove of incriminating documents. The evidence was damning—emails, financial transactions, and records of secret meetings that linked Anthony Winters directly to Nathaniel Blackwood's plan to take control of Montgomery Industries.

Emma's hands trembled with a mix of fear and determination. "We have what we need to expose Winters and Blackwood, but we can't do it alone. We need to rally support within the company and present this evidence to the board."

Mark nodded in agreement. "We should approach trusted members of the board who have shown resistance to Blackwood's agenda. With this evidence, we might be able to sway their support."

Sarah, her gaze locked on the screens, added, "And we need to do it quickly. Blackwood won't sit idly by once he realizes we have this information."

Their plan was set in motion. Over the next few days, they discreetly reached out to board members who had expressed concerns about the proposed merger and Blackwood's influence. The evidence they presented was compelling, leaving no room for doubt about Winters' and Blackwood's nefarious scheme.

As the board meeting approached, tensions within Montgomery Industries reached a fever pitch. Rumors swirled, and the battle lines were drawn. The fate of the company hung in the balance, and the showdown between those who sought to protect its integrity and those who aimed to exploit it was imminent.

The day of the board meeting arrived, and the tension in the air was palpable. Emma, Mark, and Sarah sat in the boardroom, their hearts pounding as they awaited the moment of reckoning. The evidence they had gathered weighed heavily on their minds, and the outcome of this pivotal meeting would determine the fate of Montgomery Industries.

The board members filed into the room, their expressions a mix of curiosity and apprehension. Anthony Winters and Nathaniel Blackwood were also present, their faces masks of confidence that belied the storm brewing beneath the surface.

Emma rose to her feet, her voice steady and resolute, as she presented the evidence of Winters' and Blackwood's collusion. The room fell silent as board members examined the documents and emails that left no doubt about the sinister plot to take over the company.

Winters and Blackwood exchanged uneasy glances as their defense crumbled under the weight of the evidence. The board members, once divided, began to shift their allegiance, recognizing the gravity of the situation.

In a climactic moment, a board member who had previously supported Blackwood stood up and declared, "I can no longer condone this unethical behavior. I move to reject the proposed merger and remove Anthony Winters from the board."

The room erupted into a chorus of agreement, and the balance of power shifted decisively in favor of those who sought to protect the company's integrity.

As the meeting concluded, Winters and Blackwood were escorted out of the boardroom, their plan foiled, their ambitions shattered. Emma, Mark, and Sarah watched in silence as justice prevailed, and Montgomery Industries was saved from the brink of destruction.

Their journey had been fraught with danger and uncertainty, but they had uncovered the truth and exposed the conspirators who had threatened the company. The battle was won, but the scars of the corporate espionage they had endured would forever remind them of the price of justice.

As they left the boardroom, the weight of their victory and the knowledge that they had safeguarded Montgomery Industries filled them with a sense of accomplishment and pride. They knew that the road ahead would be filled with challenges, but they were prepared to face whatever lay ahead, united in their commitment to protect the company they held dear.

The chapter closed on a suspenseful note, but it was a chapter that had ended in triumph, a testament to the power of determination, integrity, and unwavering resolve in the face of corporate intrigue and deception.

# Unfinished Business

With the expulsion of Anthony Winters and Nathaniel Blackwood from the boardroom of Montgomery Industries, a tense calm settled over the corporate landscape. The threat that had loomed over the company had been averted, but the aftermath of the battle left behind a complex web of consequences and unfinished business.

Emma Montgomery sat in her office, the weight of the recent events pressing down on her shoulders. The morning sun streamed in through the window, casting a warm glow on the polished wooden desk, but the sense of unease lingered. The victory had come at a cost, and there were still unanswered questions that gnawed at her.

Mark Reynolds entered her office, his face bearing the weight of the unfinished business that lay ahead. "Emma, we can't let our guard down. Blackwood may be gone, but there are lingering traces of his influence within the company. We need to root out any remaining collaborators."

Emma nodded in agreement. "You're right, Mark. We can't afford to become complacent. We need to conduct a thorough internal audit and ensure that our board members are committed to the company's well-being."

Their conversation was interrupted by a knock on the door. It was Sarah Dawson, her expression troubled. "Emma, Mark, I've been doing some digging, and I found something concerning. It appears that Blackwood had other interests and connections outside of Montgomery Industries."

Mark arched an eyebrow. "What kind of interests are we talking about?"

Sarah shared her findings, revealing that Blackwood had been involved in a web of financial dealings that extended beyond their initial investigation. It seemed that Blackwood's influence reached far and wide, and his connections ran deep within the world of corporate espionage.

Emma's eyes narrowed with concern. "If Blackwood had other schemes in motion, we need to uncover them. We can't allow his legacy of deceit to persist."

Mark agreed. "We should contact the authorities and provide them with the evidence we have. Let them pursue any criminal charges against Blackwood and his associates."

As they prepared to take the next steps in their ongoing battle, the trio couldn't help but feel a lingering sense of unease. Blackwood's shadow had cast a long, dark pall over their lives, and they knew that the consequences of their actions would ripple far beyond the walls of Montgomery Industries.

In the weeks that followed, the investigation into Nathaniel Blackwood's criminal network intensified. Emma, Mark, and Sarah worked closely with law enforcement agencies, sharing the evidence they had gathered and helping to dismantle the intricate web of deceit that Blackwood had woven.

It was during this time that they received an unexpected visitor. The masked figure who had provided them with crucial information in the abandoned subway station had returned, this time with a message of gratitude.

"I wanted to thank you for exposing Blackwood's schemes," the figure said, their voice no longer distorted by the mask. "You've done a great service, not just for Montgomery Industries, but for many others who were affected by his actions."

Emma was curious. "Who are you, and why did you help us?"

The figure revealed their identity as an investigative journalist who had been working undercover to expose Blackwood's criminal activities for years. "I couldn't do it alone, and your determination to uncover the truth aligned with my own mission. Together, we were able to expose the corruption that ran deep within the corporate world."

With the journalist's assistance, Blackwood's criminal network was further dismantled, and more individuals were brought to justice. It became clear that their actions had far-reaching implications, affecting not only Montgomery Industries but the entire financial landscape of the city.

As the dust settled on their long and arduous battle, Emma, Mark, and Sarah couldn't help but reflect on the journey they had undertaken. They had faced danger, deception, and uncertainty, but they had emerged victorious, bringing the perpetrators to justice and safeguarding the integrity of Montgomery Industries.

Their bond, forged in the crucible of corporate espionage, remained unbreakable, and they knew that their work was far from over. The corporate world was a place of constant change and challenge, and they were prepared to face whatever lay ahead, armed with the lessons they had learned and the strength of their convictions.

The chapter closed not with a sense of finality, but with the understanding that in the world of corporate intrigue, there would always be unfinished business, new challenges, and hidden threats waiting to be uncovered. Emma, Mark, and Sarah were ready for whatever lay ahead, united in their commitment to protect the legacy of Montgomery Industries and to seek justice in a world where the line between right and wrong was often blurred.

# Shadows of Resurgence

The passage of time had brought a semblance of normalcy back to Montgomery Industries. With the removal of Anthony Winters and Nathaniel Blackwood, the company's operations had stabilized, and the board was now focused on rebuilding trust and ensuring the company's long-term success. Emma Montgomery, Mark Reynolds, and Sarah Dawson had resumed their respective roles within the company, but the memories of their harrowing battle against corporate espionage still haunted their every move.

In the heart of Montgomery Industries' sleek and modern headquarters, Emma sat in her corner office, her gaze fixed on the city skyline beyond the floor-to-ceiling windows. The room, bathed in the soft glow of afternoon sunlight, bore witness to the tumultuous events that had transpired within its walls. Emma's thoughts were a whirlwind of reflection, and she couldn't help but wonder whether they had truly eradicated the shadows that had threatened the company.

Mark entered her office, a stack of documents in hand, and broke her reverie. "Emma, we've been making progress in strengthening our internal controls and governance, but there's still work to be done. We can't afford to let our guard down."

Emma nodded, her eyes returning to the documents before her. "You're right,

Mark. Blackwood's influence ran deep, and we need to ensure that every trace of his network has been eliminated."

As they delved into their work, Sarah joined them via video conference, her face appearing on a large screen in Emma's office. "I've been monitoring online chatter, and there are rumblings about a resurgence of corporate espionage activity in the city. It's as if someone is trying to fill the void left by Blackwood."

Mark's brows furrowed. "Could it be that some of Blackwood's associates are regrouping?"

Sarah shook her head. "It's difficult to say for sure, but we can't ignore the signs. We need to remain vigilant and keep our investigative skills sharp."

Their conversation was interrupted by a knock on the door. Emma's assistant, Alex, entered the room, a look of concern on his face. "I'm sorry to interrupt, but there's someone here to see you, Emma. He claims to have information related to Blackwood's associates."

Emma exchanged a surprised glance with Mark and Sarah before instructing Alex to bring the visitor in. Moments later, a middle-aged man in a dark suit entered the office. His eyes held a hint of weariness, as if he had been carrying a heavy burden.

"I apologize for the intrusion, Ms. Montgomery," he began, "but my name is Daniel Foster. I used to work closely with Nathaniel Blackwood and his associates."

Emma and her team exchanged cautious glances. This unexpected visitor could hold the key to uncovering any remnants of Blackwood's network.

Mark leaned forward, his voice measured. "What can you tell us, Mr. Foster?"

Daniel took a deep breath. "After Blackwood's downfall, I decided to distance myself from his criminal activities. But I couldn't live with the guilt any longer. I have information about a new group of operatives who have taken up where Blackwood left off. They're operating in the shadows, targeting major corporations, and they're ruthless."

Sarah's eyes narrowed. "Do you have evidence to support these claims?"

Daniel handed over a flash drive containing a trove of documents, emails, and encrypted files. "I've been collecting this information in secret. It exposes the activities of this new group, their targets, and their methods. I want to make amends for my past actions."

Emma's heart went out to Daniel, recognizing the weight of his decision to come forward. "Thank you, Mr. Foster. Your information is invaluable. We'll ensure it's put to good use."

As Daniel left her office, Emma couldn't help but feel a renewed sense of purpose. The battle against corporate espionage was far from over, and their commitment to justice remained steadfast. They had faced the shadows once before and emerged victorious, but now a new threat lurked in the darkness, and they were determined to confront it head-on.

Over the following weeks, Emma, Mark, and Sarah meticulously analyzed the information provided by Daniel Foster. It revealed a complex web of operatives, hidden financial transactions, and a pattern of attacks on major corporations across the city. The new group seemed to be just as cunning and elusive as Blackwood's network had been.

They decided to take their findings to the authorities, providing them with the evidence they needed to launch an investigation into this resurgent threat. The battle had shifted from the boardrooms to the shadows, and they knew that dismantling this new network would require a different kind of strategy.

As they worked alongside law enforcement agencies, their days were filled with a sense of urgency and determination. The investigation intensified, uncovering connections between the new operatives and high-ranking officials in the corporate world. The fight against corporate espionage was proving to be a formidable and dangerous adversary.

One evening, as Emma, Mark, and Sarah gathered in Emma's office to discuss their progress, a message arrived. It was a video message from an anonymous source, showing a shadowed figure addressing the camera.

"We are the architects of chaos," the figure declared. "We will expose the corruption and greed that

plagues the corporate world. You may have defeated Blackwood, but we are a new breed, and we are unstoppable."

The video ended abruptly, leaving an eerie silence in its wake.

Emma clenched her fists, her voice determined. "We won't be intimidated. We'll uncover the truth and bring these criminals to justice, just as we did before."

The shadows of resurgence had cast a dark cloud over their lives, but Emma, Mark, and Sarah were prepared to face the challenge head-on. The battle against corporate espionage continued, and they would not rest until the perpetrators were unmasked and the world of business was free from the looming threat of darkness.

As the chapter came to a close, the trio braced themselves for the storm that lay ahead, knowing that the shadows of the past had returned with a vengeance, and their determination to seek justice burned brighter than ever before.

# The Web Tightens

As the investigation into the resurgent threat of corporate espionage continued, Montgomery Industries became a fortress of vigilance. Emma Montgomery, Mark Reynolds, and Sarah Dawson worked tirelessly alongside law enforcement agencies to uncover the identities of the new operatives and dismantle their shadowy network.

Late one evening, in Sarah's cluttered but meticulously organized apartment, the trio gathered around a table stacked with documents, laptops, and monitors displaying encrypted files. The walls bore charts and timelines mapping out the activities of the operatives, their connections, and potential targets.

Sarah's fingers flew across the keyboard as she attempted to crack one of the encrypted files. "This is some next-level encryption, but I'm close. I can feel it."

Mark leaned forward, scrutinizing the evidence. "We need a breakthrough, something that ties these operatives to their true identities. Without that, we're fighting in the dark."

Emma, her eyes fixed on the screen, couldn't shake the feeling that the new operatives were always one step ahead. "We need to anticipate their moves, figure out their patterns. There must be something we're missing."

Their conversation was interrupted by a knock at the door. Startled, they exchanged uneasy glances. Sarah cautiously approached the door and peered through the peephole, then let out a sigh of relief. "It's just Daniel Foster."

Daniel entered, his face etched with worry. "I've been keeping an eye on the new operatives, and it seems they're planning a major operation. They're targeting a tech conglomerate in the city."

Emma's heart sank. "Do you have any details, Daniel?"

He nodded, sharing the information he had gathered. "Their plan involves infiltrating the company's servers to steal sensitive data, and it's set to happen in two days."

Mark's jaw clenched with determination. "We can't let this happen. We need to stop them before they succeed."

They agreed to combine their efforts to thwart the impending attack. Emma contacted the authorities, sharing the information they had, while Mark and Sarah continued to analyze the evidence. The countdown to the operation had begun, and they knew they were racing against time.

Two days later, they stood in a dimly lit alley outside the tech conglomerate's headquarters. The night was overcast, the air heavy with tension. Emma, Mark, Sarah, and a team of law enforcement officers were on high alert, ready to intercept the operatives and protect the company's data.

Sarah's phone buzzed with an urgent message. She glanced at the screen and relayed the information to the team. "The operatives are approaching from the east side of the building. It's time."

As they moved into position, their hearts pounded with a mix of apprehension and determination. The moment had come to confront the new threat head-on, to expose the shadows that had resurged with a vengeance.

The operatives, clad in black attire and wearing masks, crept closer to the building's entrance. Their movements were precise, their intentions clear. They aimed to breach the security measures and gain access to the company's servers.

Emma and Mark, concealed in the shadows, watched as the operatives approached the entrance. They signaled to the law enforcement team, who moved in to intercept the intruders.

A tense standoff ensued, the operatives outnumbered and outmaneuvered. The law enforcement team had the element of surprise on their side, and the operatives were quickly apprehended.

As the operatives were escorted away in handcuffs, their masks removed to reveal their faces, a sense of satisfaction washed over Emma, Mark, and Sarah. The battle was far from over, but they had successfully thwarted the attack and exposed the operatives' identities.

In the aftermath, they interrogated the captured operatives, determined to uncover the mastermind behind the resurgent threat. The operatives, faced with the weight of their actions, began to divulge information.

It was revealed that the new group of operatives had been led by a mysterious figure known only as "The Orchestrator." The Orchestrator had recruited individuals from various backgrounds, each with unique skills and expertise, to carry out a series of high-profile corporate attacks.

Emma couldn't help but wonder about the identity of this enigmatic leader. "Do you have any information on The Orchestrator's true identity?"

One of the captured operatives hesitated before speaking. "We never met The Orchestrator in person. All communication was done through encrypted channels. We don't know who they are, but they're brilliant at covering their tracks."

Mark exchanged a glance with Emma. The Orchestrator remained a shadowy figure, and unraveling their true identity seemed like an insurmountable challenge.

In the weeks that followed, Montgomery Industries continued to strengthen its internal controls, and the city's law enforcement agencies worked diligently to dismantle the remnants of the operatives' network. The battle against corporate espionage had taken another turn, and the web of deceit and intrigue continued to tighten.

Late one evening, as Emma, Mark, and Sarah gathered once again in Sarah's apartment, they couldn't help but reflect on the journey they had undertaken. They had faced danger, deception, and the resurgence of a powerful adversary, but they had emerged victorious once more.

Sarah, her voice filled with determination, broke the silence. "We may not have unmasked The Orchestrator yet, but we've shown that they can be defeated. We'll continue to expose their network and protect the corporate world from their reign of chaos."

Emma and Mark nodded in agreement, their bond stronger than ever. The battle against corporate espionage was ongoing, and they knew that their commitment to justice was unwavering. The shadows might resurge, but they were ready to face whatever challenges lay ahead, united in their mission to seek the truth and safeguard the world of business from the darkness that threatened to engulf it.

# The Orchestrator's Gambit

In the heart of the city, amid the towering skyscrapers that symbolized its corporate might, Emma Montgomery, Mark Reynolds, and Sarah Dawson continued their relentless pursuit of justice. The resurgent threat of corporate espionage had forced them to remain vigilant, and the shadowy figure known as "The Orchestrator" remained an elusive adversary, lurking in the shadows.

One crisp autumn morning, Emma received an encrypted email on her secure server. The subject line simply read, "The Orchestrator's Gambit." She knew that this message could hold the key to unmasking their enigmatic adversary. Her heart raced as she decrypted the message, revealing its contents.

The email contained a cryptic message, written in a code that was both intricate and maddeningly puzzling. It hinted at an upcoming operation, one that would have far-reaching consequences for the corporate world. The Orchestrator's gambit was in motion, and Emma, Mark, and Sarah were determined to decipher its meaning.

As they gathered in Sarah's apartment to analyze the message, frustration and anticipation hung in the air like a dense fog. Sarah projected the encrypted message onto a screen, her fingers poised over the keyboard.

"This code is unlike anything we've encountered before," Sarah admitted, her brow furrowed. "It's as if The Orchestrator has designed it to be impenetrable."

Mark nodded in agreement, his gaze fixed on the screen. "We need to break this code. It's our only lead to uncovering their plan."

Hours turned into days as they tirelessly worked to decipher the message. They tried various decryption techniques, cross-referencing the symbols and patterns with known codes, but The Orchestrator's cunning proved to be a formidable adversary.

One evening, as they sat amidst a sea of discarded code-breaking attempts, a breakthrough occurred. Sarah, her eyes wide with realization, pointed to a section of the message. "I think I've found a pattern, a recurring sequence of symbols that appears to be a key."

Emma leaned in, her heart pounding with excitement. "If that's the key, then it could unlock the rest of the message."

Mark, his fingers poised over the keyboard, began to rearrange the symbols according to the pattern they had identified. As the code fell into place, a message slowly emerged.

"It's a location," Mark announced, his voice tinged with urgency. "The message points to an abandoned industrial facility on the outskirts of the city. That's where The Orchestrator's gambit is set to unfold."

They knew they couldn't waste any time. The impending operation had to be stopped, and The Orchestrator had to be unmasked. With the location in hand, they contacted the authorities and prepared to investigate the abandoned facility.

The night was dark and filled with an eerie silence as they approached the industrial facility. The air was thick with tension, and the shadows seemed to dance in the dim moonlight. Armed with flashlights and determination, they ventured inside, the echo of their footsteps a haunting reminder of the uncertainty that lay ahead.

The facility was a labyrinthine maze of corridors, rusted machinery, and long-forgotten equipment. Their flashlights revealed traces of recent activity—footprints, discarded tools, and cryptic symbols painted on the walls.

Sarah's voice trembled as she pointed to one of the symbols. "This matches the pattern from The Orchestrator's message. We're on the right track."

As they delved deeper into the facility, they came upon a chamber that seemed to be the epicenter of The Orchestrator's operation. Computer servers hummed with activity, and screens displayed intricate diagrams and plans.

Mark's eyes widened as he examined the data. "They were planning a massive cyberattack, one that would cripple the financial infrastructure of the city. It's a coordinated assault on major corporations."

The implications of The Orchestrator's plan sent shivers down their spines. It was a gambit that threatened to plunge the entire city into chaos, with far-reaching consequences for the corporate world.

But there was no sign of The Orchestrator themselves. They had slipped through their fingers once again, leaving behind only a cryptic message that taunted their pursuers.

As they left the abandoned facility, their mission far from complete, Emma couldn't help but feel a sense of frustration and determination. The Orchestrator remained a shadowy figure, always one step ahead, but they were determined to unmask this enigmatic adversary and bring them to justice.

Back in Sarah's apartment, they worked tirelessly to analyze the data they had gathered from the facility. It revealed a complex network of operatives, each with a specific role to play in The Orchestrator's gambit. But the identity of The Orchestrator themselves remained a mystery, hidden behind layers of encryption and anonymity.

Emma, her voice filled with resolve, addressed her companions. "We can't let The Orchestrator succeed. We need to gather all the evidence we have and share it with the authorities. We'll work together to stop this cyberattack and expose the mastermind behind it."

As they continued their investigation and prepared to thwart The Orchestrator's gambit, a sense of urgency filled the air. The city's financial infrastructure hung in the balance, and the shadows of corporate espionage had once again cast a long and ominous pall over their lives.

The chapter closed with a sense of foreboding, as Emma, Mark, and Sarah braced themselves for the final confrontation with The Orchestrator, determined to bring an end to their reign of chaos and unmask the true face of their formidable adversary.

# Unmasking the Orchestrator

The clock ticked relentlessly as the investigation into The Orchestrator's gambit reached a critical juncture. Emma Montgomery, Mark Reynolds, and Sarah Dawson had gathered their evidence, working tirelessly to thwart the impending cyberattack that threatened the city's financial infrastructure. The elusive figure known as The Orchestrator remained their primary target, and they were determined to unmask the mastermind behind the chaos that loomed on the horizon.

In a high-tech surveillance room within Montgomery Industries, they huddled around a bank of monitors displaying a live feed of the industrial facility they had discovered—the same facility where The Orchestrator's operation had been set in motion. Law enforcement officers, tech experts, and analysts worked diligently, preparing for the imminent confrontation.

Sarah's voice broke the tense silence as she updated the team. "We've identified the key operatives behind The Orchestrator's cyberattack. They're coordinating from within that facility."

Mark nodded, his eyes fixed on the monitors. "We need to move in before they can execute their plan. Time is running out."

Emma, her gaze never leaving the screens, addressed the law enforcement team. "Prepare to raid the facility. Our priority is to apprehend The Orchestrator and secure any evidence we can find."

As they readied themselves for the operation, a sense of urgency filled the room. The fate of the city's financial infrastructure hung in the balance, and they knew that they were racing against time to thwart The Orchestrator's gambit.

The raid on the industrial facility unfolded with precision and determination. Law enforcement officers, armed with tactical gear, breached the facility's defenses while tech experts attempted to disable the cyberattack in progress.

Emma, Mark, and Sarah, accompanied by a team of officers, entered the facility. The air was thick with tension as they navigated the labyrinthine corridors, following the trail of evidence that had led them here.

As they ventured deeper into the facility, they encountered resistance from The Orchestrator's operatives. A fierce firefight erupted, echoing through the metal corridors. The operatives, clad in black, fought with a desperate resolve, determined to protect their nefarious leader.

Amidst the chaos of the firefight, Emma spotted a figure in the distance—a shadowy silhouette watching the battle unfold. It was The Orchestrator, their identity still concealed behind a mask and hood.

Mark and Sarah provided cover fire as Emma pursued The Orchestrator, determined to unmask them and bring an end to their reign of chaos. The chase led them through a maze of corridors, each turn taking them deeper into the facility's bowels.

Finally, in a dimly lit chamber filled with humming servers, Emma cornered The Orchestrator. The figure turned to face her, their mask concealing their identity. A tense silence hung in the air as Emma's eyes locked onto The

Orchestrator.

"Your gambit ends here," Emma declared, her voice unwavering.

The Orchestrator's voice was distorted, a chilling blend of determination and defiance. "You may have thwarted this operation, but chaos cannot be stopped. The corporate world is a cesspool of greed and corruption, and I am its reckoning."

With a swift movement, Emma lunged at The Orchestrator, their struggle intensifying. The mask slipped, revealing a glimpse of the figure's face, but they fought fiercely to maintain their anonymity.

As the struggle continued, Mark and Sarah burst into the chamber, their guns drawn. The Orchestrator's resistance faltered, and they were apprehended, their identity finally exposed to the world.

The shock of revelation filled the room as the mask was removed, revealing the face of a high-ranking executive from a rival tech conglomerate. The Orchestrator's true identity sent shockwaves through the corporate world, exposing a web of deceit and betrayal that ran deeper than anyone had imagined.

With The Orchestrator in custody and their operation thwarted, the city's financial infrastructure was safe once more. The resurgent threat of corporate espionage had been vanquished, and justice had been served.

Back in Sarah's apartment, Emma, Mark, and Sarah reflected on the events that had transpired. The battle against The Orchestrator had been a long and treacherous journey, but they had emerged victorious, unmasking the true face of their formidable adversary.

Sarah, her voice filled with conviction, spoke first. "We've shown that even the most cunning of adversaries can be defeated. The corporate world may have its shadows, but we will always seek the truth and protect those who are vulnerable to its darkness."

Mark nodded in agreement. "Our mission isn't just about corporate espionage; it's about justice and integrity. We'll continue to expose corruption wherever it exists."

Emma, a sense of fulfillment washing over her, concluded, "The battle may be ongoing, but we've proven that the forces of good can triumph over the forces of darkness. The legacy of Montgomery Industries will always be one of integrity and justice."

As the chapter came to a close, a new sense of purpose filled the room. The shadows of corporate espionage had been banished, and Emma, Mark, and Sarah knew that their commitment to justice would guide them through whatever challenges lay ahead. The world of business would always have its secrets, but they were ready to face them head-on, united in their mission to seek the truth and protect the corporate world from the darkness that threatened to engulf it.

# The Legacy of Shadows

In the wake of their triumphant unmasking of The Orchestrator and the dismantling of the resurgent threat of corporate espionage, Montgomery Industries stood as a symbol of resilience and integrity in the corporate world. Emma Montgomery, Mark Reynolds, and Sarah Dawson had emerged from the shadows, their bond forged through the crucible of relentless pursuit of justice. However, even as they celebrated their victories, they knew that the legacy of shadows would forever linger in the corridors of power.

Within the pristine walls of Montgomery Industries, Emma sat in her corner office, her gaze fixed on the city skyline beyond the floor-to-ceiling windows. The sun cast long shadows, reminding her of the darkness they had confronted and the relentless pursuit of truth that had driven them.

Mark entered her office, a smile playing on his lips. "Emma, it's been a year since we unmasked The Orchestrator. The corporate world has changed. Transparency and accountability are no longer just buzzwords; they're guiding principles."

Emma nodded, her voice filled with pride. "Our battle against corporate espionage brought about a paradigm shift. Montgomery Industries has become a beacon of hope, and other corporations are following suit. But the shadows are always lurking."

Their conversation was interrupted by a knock at the door. It was Sarah, her expression thoughtful. "I've been monitoring online chatter, and there are whispers of a new figure emerging in the world of corporate espionage. They're calling themselves 'The Reckoner.'"

Mark raised an eyebrow. "The Reckoner? Could it be that The Orchestrator had an apprentice or protege?"

Sarah shared her findings, revealing that The Reckoner had been responsible for a series of high-profile data breaches and leaks, exposing corporate wrongdoing on a grand scale. It seemed that the legacy of shadows had given rise to a new force that sought to expose the sins of the corporate world.

Emma's curiosity was piqued. "What's their motive, Sarah?"

Sarah scrolled through her tablet, displaying snippets of The Reckoner's manifesto. "They claim to be the reckoning for corporate greed and corruption. They believe that transparency is the only path to a just and equitable world."

Mark leaned forward, intrigued. "So, they're acting as vigilantes of sorts, exposing the darkest secrets of corporations."

As they continued to discuss The Reckoner's activities, a sense of unease settled over the room. The new figure was operating with a different agenda, one that blurred the line between hero and vigilante. It was a challenge that demanded their attention and vigilance.

Over the following weeks, Montgomery Industries became the target of The Reckoner's scrutiny. Their confidential documents and internal communications were leaked, exposing the company's vulnerabilities and shortcomings. It was a stark reminder that the shadows of corporate espionage could never truly be banished.

Emma, Mark, and Sarah worked tirelessly to fortify the company's defenses, but The Reckoner proved to be a formidable adversary. Each move they made was met with a countermove, and the battle for corporate transparency intensified.

One evening, as they gathered in a secure meeting room within the company, Emma voiced her concerns. "The Reckoner's actions are forcing us to confront our own vulnerabilities and strive for greater transparency. But their methods are extreme, and they risk causing chaos in the corporate world."

Mark nodded in agreement. "We need to find a way to reason with The Reckoner, to show them that there are more constructive ways to bring about change."

Sarah, her gaze thoughtful, added, "We also need to consider the possibility that The Reckoner might have valid grievances. We can't dismiss their actions entirely."

Their conversation was interrupted by a notification on Sarah's tablet. It was a message from The Reckoner, requesting a meeting. They were willing to engage in a dialogue.

Emma, Mark, and Sarah agreed to meet The Reckoner in person, understanding that this encounter could shape the future of corporate transparency and accountability. The meeting was arranged at an undisclosed location, far from the prying eyes of the corporate world.

As they entered a dimly lit, underground chamber, a figure clad in a black hooded cloak awaited them. The Reckoner's face was concealed, their identity hidden in the shadows.

Emma stepped forward, her voice steady. "We're here to understand your motives and goals. We believe in transparency and accountability, but your methods are causing chaos."

The Reckoner's voice, distorted to conceal their identity, echoed through the chamber. "The corporate world is a breeding ground for greed and corruption. Change must come from within, but the shadows persist. My actions are a reckoning for those who exploit their power."

Mark, his voice measured, responded, "We agree that change is needed, but we also believe that there are more constructive ways to achieve it. Let us work together to hold corporations accountable without resorting to chaos."

The Reckoner considered their words, the weight of their actions hanging in the air. Finally, they spoke, their voice filled with uncertainty. "I will consider your offer. But the shadows of the past have left scars that run deep."

As they left the underground chamber, Emma, Mark, and Sarah knew that the battle for corporate transparency would continue. The Reckoner remained an enigmatic force, torn between their desire for justice and the chaos they had unleashed.

Back at Montgomery Industries, they resumed their mission to fortify the company's defenses and advocate for greater transparency in the corporate world. The legacy of shadows would always linger, but they were determined to ensure that the pursuit of truth and justice prevailed.

The chapter closed with a sense of uncertainty, as Emma, Mark, and Sarah faced the complex challenge of engaging with The Reckoner and navigating the shifting landscape of corporate accountability. The shadows may never truly dissipate, but their unwavering commitment to justice would guide them through the ever-changing world of business.

www.ingramcontent.com/pod-product-compliance
Ingram Content Group UK Ltd.
Pitfield, Milton Keynes, MK11 3LW, UK
UKHW020244240426
12048UKWH00026B/1603